SALT PIER

PITT POETRY SERIES

Ed Ochester, Editor

SALT PIER

DORE KIESSELBACH

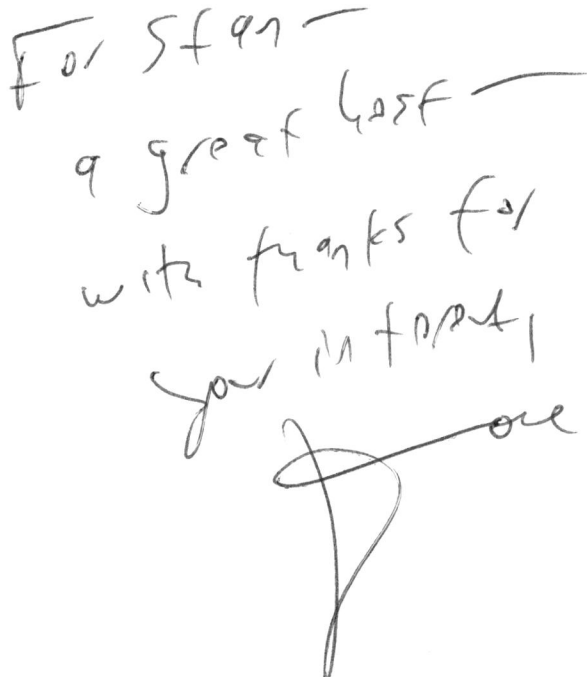

For Stan —
a great host —
with thanks for
your interest,
Dore

University of Pittsburgh Press

Published by the University of Pittsburgh Press, Pittsburgh, Pa., 15260

Copyright © 2012, Dore Kiesselbach

All rights reserved

Manufactured in the United States of America

Printed on acid-free paper

10 9 8 7 6 5 4 3 2 1

ISBN 13: 978-0-8229-6217-5

ISBN 10: 0-8229-6217-9

For Karin, candor and joy

Repeat their semblance often on the seas

—1 *HENRY VI*, 5.5

You can hone a blade until there is no blade

—FRANZ WRIGHT

CONTENTS

✻

✻ ✻

CLEAVE

Close to the city, a deer
leaves a hoofprint
in our yard. I study it
under the box elder.
Speechless lips pressed
into snow if man was not
already the beast
that walks on its mouth.
I use your being
on the phone
to keep it to myself.
As if too much knowing
could drive it away.
The law says
we owned it while
it stayed with us—
what came from woods
while under wool
we twitched, pranced
a circle where next
solstice it will eat,
then left us
for the stream one
block away.
When a person says
forgive me
the please is implied.
Folding and unfolding
a slender,
black-tipped leg
it widened there
a small hole in the ice.

ORNAMENT

The Christmas tree comes down
but isn't dead yet, doesn't
drain the quart a day it did
the week I sawed it
from its future in the earth,
but still sips, last cells
stubborn in a local life.
Losing needles all the way,
I haul it bottom first
through the dining room,
leaving marks beside
marks I left last year
and years before,
yank yank *yank* it
out the kitchen door.
I don't believe in Santa
but I can't take it to the curb—
it brought us together
in honest wonder
on the couch.
To leave it upright
in a drift between
dangling suet
and the surveyed line
I tow it through
the yard by limbs
where varnished
feathers shined.

THE PAINTED HALL, LASCAUX

Mineral sweat beads patches of the ceiling
of *the Sistine Chapel of paleolithic*
cave art—calcium carbonate
crystallized in hexagons
flint tools couldn't smooth.
In what depends on art,
absence must be chosen
not imposed,
so the painter put
the pigment in his mouth—
manganese, toxic in high
doses, for black
and brown, iron oxide
for red ocher—mixed it,
bitterer than March grass
cropped through snow,
with saliva,
sent it to the stone
in tonguey bursts,
the roughness he covered
with his own wet self
chemically identical
to the bones of what
his color led him through.

THE CONVERGENCE
OF THE ANIMALS

is a winter custom here:
a giant puppet wolf set
in woods beside the path.
Its pine frame is padded,
will hold two humans soon.
They'll don and walk it east
to the hard center of a lake,
dance with other totems
there—elk, bear, and one
we haven't seen—come
from sister compass points.
Scattering frozen leaves
and snow the dog
barks and charges,
barks and flees a beast
so intent on destruction
it won't turn its head.
We watch from the far
side of papier-mâché
haunches set to spring.
The wolf didn't lunge
at us when we passed
but we slipped a little
near the mouth the way
couples holding hands
and roped climbers do.
(My part is to stumble,
yours to hold the line.)
When the leash man

can't soothe the dog,
he lets himself be led
back the way he came,
to safety, but first
he shows us his and
we bare our canines.

NONINVASIVE

Deciding where to put you, we speak of size
we won't live to see. It's the overhead
wires we're concerned about.
We make space by killing what was there
with poison painted on a welling stump,
amend the hole with peat when I reach clay.
That they'll be ready to connect,
she roughs your roots up,
the way doubt cultivates us,
while I hold you by the slow
persistence of your trunk.
Like a femur, we install you
in the dark hip of earth.
As I appraise your angle
to a beam and nimbus sky,
tricks of light afford
a stranger on the patio,
looking over here
when you're full grown.
I don't envy him but wonder
what he thinks of what
he sees—did we achieve
our woodland paradise?
Bending low to form
a raised soil circle for water
I'll pour each day around you
for weeks, my hands assume
that basic shape related to
but more perfect than applause.

TURKEYS ON THE PATIO

They curl a sound through morning trees
watching me distribute
their daily safflower seeds.
I'm late. They wait,
nine chicks grown two
feet tall in fifteen weeks
and she who stood
between our breakfast
window and their practice
scratch-and-pecks.
In minutes they excavate
a garden bed, gulping
raw what scurries
in scraped light
while she moves
among them, taller
by a head. In fall's
ballroom they bow
and straighten, straighten,
bow, and finish
with a salad course,
stretching for clematis
growing barer
from the bottom
and, once they learn
to leap the garden
structure, from the top.
They harry squirrels,
they stalk a cat.
Beckoned by woods,
they leave a tussled

feather we add
to wiltless others
in a low, clay pot.

RAKE

My inspiration is the turkey tail.
My verb is sexual.
I touch death
that life may be revealed
in green stupidity. I'd
love to crawl up
in the tree I owe
existence to and sleep
with leaves
before they fall.
Sometimes what
I've gathered
stays attached
to me. Some places
my crippled fingers
don't belong.
Alone I make
them fluent
as underwater hair.
All else
being equal
my effectiveness
is a function
of how far
who's using me
can reach.

SEVER

We're not killing you today but you shake
the carrier's gate as if certain otherwise.
The latch, at last you fathom, is no
problem you can solve. You turn
to me from the passenger seat,
yowl through slats in the plastic box,
deliberate as I've seen you, bell-
bestrewed, stalk juncos in the yard.
I tell you I agree—if tumor plus
incarceration plus winter morning cold
don't sum enough to gripe about,
nothing would. But intercession
not commiseration's what you seek:
again you make liquid darkness
with your tongue. With your pelvis
now in play, our best hope's
they simply *disarticulate* the leg
you can't straighten anymore.
You don't count body parts,
I'm told, won't miss it after awhile.
I look away, consider what
for me's as a leap to you, think
of losing half that strength,
of trying to forget what I could do.

GRUNION

The moon has cut the bulging coinpurse of the sea.
Up and down the coast
for miles silver fish flow
by thousands onto sand
and thrash the slick
sheen there to foam,
burying their heritage
between two domains.
Their task is engineering;
they have no mind
for what will come
to light. (It is even
possible with table
salt and tap water
to recreate that
second tide at home.)
Some of us strewn
upright in the lunar
glare register totality
on unmoving feet
while others wade
with buckets into
surf as if in a vast
dark bank vault
after the end of the world.

BALANCE

The red lion eats the green lion,
causing quite a stir
and considerable expense
to the entrepreneur who billed
the vivid cats as a spectacle
of mutant equipoise.
In silence after sirens,
under a folding chair,
he finds an unconsumed
green lion paw—spots
of green still showing
through the matted blood—
and touches it to places
he remembers having
stood while thinking
only a wonderful world
would allow a man
of his doubtful station
and low birth
to squire both
a red lion and a green lion.

It's a Tuesday

in September and as clear
as they will say.
If days had ribs
and skirts of muscle
it would be a dancing day.
In the billowing
shadow of a tall tree
a father swings his daughter
by an ankle and a wrist.
He lifts and lowers her
so she makes curving
motions in the air.
Because the world
is tilted, if he were
to let go she would
travel a long way before
touching anything.
Those of us looking up
are already there.

INFECTION

Better to stand naked
in dawn's demon grass;
dueling pistols' large-bore balls
pushed pieces of cravat, love
note, biscuit, talc, all borne
or worn accoutrement
between them and skin
into honor's sloppy room—
cologne splashed on
vertebrae, pen quills
high in humid skies, snuff
gone deeper than an addict's
dream. Pre-antisepsis,
homespun shrapnel
festered and killed
more than aim.
On its way into him,
one luckless fucker's
pocketwatch at last
told perfect time.
The outline of its crown
and stem in the edges
of the wound?
Distinct as wings
impressed
in steel and glass.

BULLET ANT

So named because its sting's akin to taking one.
4+ (highest) score
on the Schmidt Sting Pain Index.
Known in Brazil as the 24-hour ant
because the *pure, intense, brilliant*
pain of one encounter
lasts a planet-spin.
The Satere-Mawe people
soak the ants
in sedative and weave
them, sleeping,
into gloves of leaves
eased over hands of boys
who would be warriors.
They wear the gloves
for minutes
as roused ants
fire and fire again.
The hand's so full
of venom then
its arm's paralyzed
and the body
shakes for days.
Over months
they'll wear it
twenty times.
Before they may
apply pain
on the tribe's
behalf they must
for themselves
put up a great store.

GREEN ZONE

I stood at an intersection
directing traffic
and afterward told
you I felt useful.
We paid for the coffee
we drank standing,
shared a spoon.
In a window above you,
a woman smoked a cigarette,
looking over the city
into empty space
as if at a lover grown
scrutable in bliss.
A boy crossing the street
adjusted a backpack
on narrow shoulders.
A man in the crowd
spoke loudly to no one,
his face a vandalized
bicycle abandoned
with its lock.
You woke beneath stairs.
Sometimes you see
it from above.
The crumple-
zone that's death
ripples like water
toward you but stops.
I'm mixed
with prepaid phone
cards and the phone
card vendor.

Someone will have
washed them off
so they can call home.

APOLOGY

A bottle of booze rolled
out from under
the driver's seat
when you hit the brakes
hard. The special
steaks you bought
you burned. The too-
expensive toys felt wrong.
Driving us home
after a weekend visit,
going west in light
I've learned thuds
a million years
inside the sun before
happening on space,
you told us we were
more fun than
a barrelful of monkeys.
For whom is such
a monkey fun?
Mom didn't ask
too many questions.
I saw stars, breaking
the windshield
from the inside
with my head.
My apology
was sincere.
A barrel can hold
emptiness.
A barrel
can hold dread.

BASE PAIR

You said it was an accident,
a piece of glass,
that cleft your chin.
In the place before the place
before the last place,
hopelessness not yet
a tide flowing forward
when a real one
would recede, I hid
and waited. You
dropped a chicken carcass
off a wooden bridge,
returned in hours to haul
the crabs we'd have
for dinner into air.
They wouldn't let go.
Heredity's part accident
and makes the grasp
feel true. I see the gap
I didn't get from you
but not your eyes—
drawn to absolutes
for what absolution?
Home from a lab,
you threw an arm over
them, sleeping a sleep
from which at times
we couldn't wake you.
Those arms picked me
up and put me down.
I bled. Bleeding

was your specialty.
You treated a last
patient for a trait
he was born with.
Then you let go.

LADDER

The link our moms forged for us failing
after a rude death, you come to play.
I get left to my own devices a lot,
have learned to put a ladder to the roof,
scale it and transform the view.
The road to school looks less menacing
from up there, the sea shines
continuity through eucalyptus
a dozen blocks away. The power
of perspective's what I have to share
and, as you watch, to prove it,
I lean long aluminum to the eave
(but too near vertical),
take the cool rungs in my hand
and climb till I smell shingles
full of summer heat.
When I look back to see if
you're behind me with your eyes,
the turning takes me
to a fulcrum's other side.
I reach for gone gutter
through a soft spot in the air,
ascension's angle tipped
past right, oblique
and widening with speed
to spill a foregone mind.
But it's flesh and bone
not brick I hit. You're
driven to the ground,
hurt worse than I, though
we both stand up.

I'm too ashamed to speak
of it. We never speak
again. It won't occur
to me for years I didn't
crush an elbowy boy
who'd looked away.
I'll be older than my father
before I can believe
you braced yourself,
unasked, beneath my fall.

SONG

The seamstress' boy
watches his mother make
another shirt for hire.
His father gone, she looks
most familiar now
with pins in her mouth.
She wrinkles up her face
to get the sleeve straight,
wears the wrinkles
all around the house.
Alone with it one
morning he learned
the Singer's strength,
pressed the pedal,
tried to stop the belt,
the wheel, could not.
He would have tried
to stop his father too
but didn't want to know
he lacked the strength.
A silver guard is there
to keep the sewer
from the sewn.
A pocket must be
placed above the heart.

Magnifying Glass

I learn to shrink the dot until the paper
launches smoke, sizzle pistils,
wither weeds, then move
to things that move,
bring the backyard
too close to the sun
one ant at a time.
They pause as if considering
a huge question
coming from within.
When, in lieu of answering,
they roll to one side,
the wind takes them,
the way leaves blow
across the surface
of a frozen lake.

Umpire

I learn in the alley without all the rules.
There's room to plant a foot beside the road.
Good days, I paint corners with junk,
my winding up and letting go
a mash of TV righties plus
whatever else it takes to find
the flattened beer box plate.
Not even for my mother
did he bend a knee but here
who metes out punishment
calls them as they are. The things
he doesn't teach he doesn't know.

BEACH THANKSGIVING

Fire's an assortment of sparks down the beach
beside which your new family cooks.
Asked to bear a ring,
you pulled and pulled at your hair
but couldn't make yourself
presentable in the tall mirror
and went unready through
French doors into light
like that a spark might cast
if you were too small to see.
The water hauls a farther fire.
Unmoored by what almost
now caresses it, a burst
kelp bulb lolls rotting
in the lifeguard's jeep tracks.
Now you could go deep enough,
but it's too late to anchor
any father to the world.
Dodging your shadow
as you pass, a crab squints
out the attachment point
where darkness turns
to flesh, locates
its path to safety through
a seam which is neither.

QUAIL

Going where the car went
but under, not through
the guardrail,
a caravan of quail
hazards a mountain road:
mom, five chicks, then
dad in near-comic
triple-time, parents
warily swiveling
apostrophed heads,
little ones in
linearity's thrall.
If they don't keep
their heads down
they lose their
place in line.
Mid-step and breath,
you watch them
family-find green
fabric stitching
shut after being torn.

DART

You'd known me, brother, all your life
but you weren't an exile
in your own home.
Disbelief lasted one second
too long when I said
I'd throw on the count of ten.
I forget the look you gave
me just before you ran.
You nearly made the turn
at the pergola.
It was an underhand toss,
dripping spiral velocity.
Because it needed me
to fly it curved. I held
once a hummingbird,
softer than the feathers
I pulled out of you.
It had thrown itself
against a window.
It hadn't lacked the nerve.

GLASS

Staccato light
on water, a secret
language I try
deciphering
at the edge
of a park bench
after shaping putty
into windowframes
all day, the world
with me like the ghost–
pain of an amputee
who finds he can
walk on the missing
limb. Stairs
creak as I climb
to an apartment
where the wash
and layering
of recognition
has begun.
Cooling at room
temperature,
molecules
in liquid glass
bond and block
the light.
What chilled
and split us,
brother,
kept us
clear.

Aubade

Take me with you
my mother says,
standing in her nightgown
as, home from college,
I prepare to leave
before dawn.
The desolation
she must face
was once my concern
but like a bobber
pulled beneath
the surface
by an inedible fish
she vanished
into the life
he offered her.
It stopped occurring
to me she might return.
I'll be back I say
and then I go.

VOLLEY

A year or so we played every other
weekend for an hour.
I sometimes showed
a quickness that helped you hone
your game, still hear
the chainlink net's flat
rattle when struck
by your too-spun forehand.
Slurping sodas afterward
we watched ourselves
come close to chat
in a store's plate glass.
Had I been your real
son would you have gone
less frequently to the overhead?
You hated the permission
I gave myself to live,
sensing it preceded you,
a weed in the cracked court.
When you found
a better partner you
held your serves at love.
He came to your funeral,
said you'd grown close
but he feared at any
moment hearing
something unforgivable.
You told me you were
happiest with prostitutes—
sad, not terrible—but,
spoken to my mother,

your final words
were *get away*,
a shot in passing,
down the line, that
couldn't be returned.

STEPFATHER

In sleep, I find you
drinking the costly whisky
I inherited when cancer
finished eating you alive.
When you open your eyes
I see straight
into flames
behind you.
You taught me to build fires,
to use an ax
in the woodpile behind the house.
I practiced chopping
off your arms
at the shoulders.
How delicate
the kindling.
How sharp
the blade.
You never fucked me
but you wanted to
and that fucked me
up. Now, the intimacy
of an accusation
brings us together.
You tell me
I'm achieving
adulthood as required
by myth. You're
dead right.

WINDMILL

Raised in a tourist town, I know
what the locals think
as we struggle to stay
upright with luggage
on the sloping gangplank.
They lounge against the hulls
of overturned smacks,
smoking, watching us pass
with slow eyes,
like cormorants tilted
toward shadows in
waves as they glide.
They've seen this march
enough to know
we'll find a room near
the center of town,
throw the windows
open to catch splashed
market sounds.
As steaming water
drums the fiberglass
shower stall and you
scrub away lotion
and brine, I'll stretch
out at an angle
on the lumpy bed,
admiring a kit
mosaic missing
enough pieces
to have left its
kitsch behind.

And when you
emerge smiling
in clean clothes
and we troop
toward brochure
vistas on the hill,
a man will sift
our things and lift
our passports,
make us citizens
of nowhere,
grain bound
for asylum
at the grinding wheel.

The Value of Literature

It rained as if each drop falling
had begged to go first,
so that the bookstore
opened its arms
like a grandmother
waiting beside her table
in the darkest
part of the wood.
You were perched
on a ladder, leafing
maps of the world.
It was impossible
not to think
of your body.
Did I need
to say a word?
Meanderers
were everywhere.
We picked
a passage
and embarked,
wrapped in coats,
against Karl Marx.

EXPRESS

The subway platform shudders as a train
comes into view, its headlight
giving girders instant life.
Across third rails,
on the inbound side, a homeless
woman's pants are down.
Between two movie posters,
beside a garbage can,
her urine splatters
the base of a tiled wall.
Impaired as she is, she makes
sure her shoes stay uninvolved.
Strangers next to me
laugh and point. God*damn*,
one says to his friend.
I'm in a suit, and a tie
so tight I could be dangling.
At the far end of the platform
tracks go overground—
light like cotton in the mouth
of an aspirin bottle.
It's a miracle drug,
I'm telling myself
as scratched plastic windows
stop-frame each of us
so fast to the other
no anima's motion's
going anywhere.

PROTECT AND SERVE

The taillights of the night's last BART train fade.
Too cheap and poor to take a cab
I choose to walk the bridge, not doubting
it was meant for what I have in mind
until the steel mesh platform
I stepped from sidewalk onto narrows
to a catwalk above the boat-lit bay.
Fat rivets and low cable
complicate the passage, but fuzzy
on the difference between *think* and *do*
I go on, not guessing what late drivers,
looking up on elevated roadways
in and out, must think. The squad
car with its lights on surprises me
as I surprise its occupants, coming
down so readily when they say.
One has seen a prostitute push
himself into air with the final
strength of legs younger than mine,
so they're gentle with me in the car.
All they do is call me *dumb fucking kid*
and once they're satisfied
that's really what I am they take me
to the Oakland side,
their jurisdiction's limit, halfway home.

WARD

It comes from darkness older than itself
and wants out. Testing us
with tiny sounds it flies a holding
pattern in the living room,
waiting for a wall to turn to night.
I quell calls for a broom,
find a plastic bag, time
a pursing snatch. With fingers
that once fastened on your throat,
I open the front door,
almost drunk enough to think
remission's in the other hand.
Before we met you burned
yourself with cigarettes.
I became your scourge.
Round and round we flew.
First to find an opening
you married someone else.
I loved the snare, not you.
Electric eyes are closing
streetlights overhead but
the bat won't ungrip all
the world it's sure of now
as I try to loose it on the lawn.
Not until I roll the bag
back upon itself, the way
a doctor's glove comes off,
and press thumbs down,
does it spill out—
wrinkled-infant face up,
gasping into fear it's hurt,
laboring against dawn.

PULP

Down to final strokes, he sees he's made
a mouth in the tree with his ax.
He's cut down hundreds.
Now this one wants to speak.
He leans his head so close to it
his ear could be its food—
the sound of wooden crickets
rubbing wings before a storm.
He extends a hand toward
pulp his swings have made,
pinches up a tangle
of moist shreds, tucks them
in his mouth like chew.
All his life he thought
it would be bitter
but it's sweet.
You are not my father
he says and takes a plug.
You are not my mother
he says and takes another.
As night pulls
higher in the leaves
he stuffs himself
until the tree falls down.

COMMUTE

On the long drive to work
I listen to radio and feel
lifted away from care.
Other drivers do well
though some are too
sudden or aggressive.
I've seen some gesture,
some make a request.
I've seen hooves
skitter on concrete.
I swerved, lost sight
of hair that came from leaves
beside the road,
then the rearview
mirror spilled its guts.
How much of what
you're breathing
was a gasp before?
Before I could drive
anywhere I learned
stones heaved high
on a winter pond
make a music move
through trees if,
between ice and silt,
enough liquid
remains to pass
the whack of impact
back and forth:
ooooo, oooo, ooo, as if

land could know
a hurt, as if land
could sing. This lane
becomes that lane
if you stay on it.

Coup de Grâce

Buckling up in the Home Depot parking lot
I see a Cooper's hawk grab lunch
from a strip-mall tree
and throttle it on the ground
while looking around
for what might steal its meat.
I'm not the only watcher—
someone hits the gas,
lunges in a welded cage
at the startled bird.
I wonder who has
touched her thus.
Accounts of people
saved from the jaws
of big cats and of child-survivors
of Mom and Pop
attacks, suggest
the sparrow's terror
has gone to drowsy
bliss. I shake
my head and make
the hands-out gesture
why'd you do that.
Like stricken wings
my hands appear
helpless to resist.

Ojibwe

On the shore of Lake Superior, south of Thunder Bay,
a tree still sacred to the local band
of what this country once called Chippewa
grows from bare rock at a promontory's tip.
(The tree doesn't grow from rock.)
Burled and bent, it's known to them as *little spirit*.
(The tree doesn't grow from rock.)
Its branches have governed lake
passage since before the fur trade.
(The tree doesn't grow from rock.)
No one walks the path to it without tribal
chaperones since outsiders wrote
their emptiness with knives on it.
(The tree doesn't grow from rock.)
In a vestibule of elements,
torsion in its trunk is seen
when spray's cold window slides.
(The tree doesn't grow from rock.)
It's called *witch tree*
in the language we and the vandals use.
Linguists say it takes around a thousand years,
the lifespan of white cedar,
to become unrecognizable.
The tree grows through the rock.

TURKEY FALLEN DEAD
FROM TREE

Startled from snow-day slumber
by a neighbor's mutt, it
banged its buzzard's head
then couldn't solve
the problem of the white
pine's limbs with wings
nearly too broad
for a planned descent.
Somewhere a lumbering
angel knows whether
it was dead before
it hit the ground.
Any sinner could tell
it was dead after—
eyes unseen beneath
bare and wrinkled lids,
feet drawn up
almost as high as hands.
I loved to watch thistle
and millet disappear
beneath it in the yard.
As snow covers
feathers that will still be
iridescent in the spring,
I remember seeing
a businessman take
a dripping handful
of pocket change
and throw it down
a subway grate

beside a homeless man.
The coins bounced
and clattered, vanishing
in the humid dark.
The rich man said
now you're having
a shitty day too.
But it's not a shitty
day and won't be
when I retrieve
the bird and walk it—
toes curling stiff
from a shopping bag—
to a houseless scrap
of oak savannah
birdseed drew it
from and dig it
into deeper snow
so what was hoarded
by a man may by
the thaw be doled.

FRAME

Calibration grows from estimation so give
the hole a decent start,
fingertip your way to a sweet spot
in the wall, nick the plaster,
raise and strike a nail.
You'll move it once you eyeball
what you hang,
then move it again
(the room requires
asymmetry, if only due to light).
Avoid philosophy but range
widely in proportion
to the boundaries you'll suspend,
that you suspend now,
pushing the out-of-sight wire
away from you so it will catch.

BOBOLI SLOPE

You remember being there
but not what it was like,
the incline of the road
to it from the river,
the press of locals
bargaining at stalls
a few blocks
from the gate,
a fee of colored
paper pushed
through a partition
with a second
hole for words—
then stone steps
flowing this way
and that, weather-
blurred animal
statuary, a hill
you climbed
in metaphor gone
literal, in bloom.

MEDICINE LAKE

I'm talking about the omen in nomenclature
when you say a single tree in Mexico
can hold 100,00 butterflies.
I'm smart enough to shut up then.
At the turn-back point of our ride,
bikes leaned against the burly
trunk of a loud-leaved oak,
we sit beside a lake, silent,
looking west as a fall sun
claims less and less of a more
and more interesting sky.
Placebo comes from the Latin
Office of the Dead. *I will*
please the Lord of the living
world, the Psalm says.
Faking history with deceaseds
for seats at Dark Age
funeral feasts made
the floating verb
a swerving noun.
But food's the other
problem now and, turning
from some broken ground,
you'll want to think
I had a secret friend—
we hear softer irony
today. I praise the role
of fiction in a migratory
life. An eagle
rides by, tall, unfeigned.

EQUALIZING

When I first saw hair loose on the back of your neck
I thought of the kind of waterfall
that can be walked behind.
My analyst told me to show you a good time.
I'd learned you loved to dive.
A week of nights when you thought
I was studying, I took the regulator
in my mouth, passed the test
with the chart turned to the wall,
then surprised you with plans for Cozumel.
Cousteau'd put it on the map
when people spoke of *frogmen*.
Remember how shot we were,
from shouldering gear, after customs,
in the cab? We leaned back
and looked through opposite
windows at jungle rolling past
like the background of a movie
with heads a little bowed to those
who stayed we still might leave.
But you were too tired to bolt
as I bribed the desk clerk
for his highest room.
We set our luggage down,
walked toward a sunlit balcony
and 5000 jigsaw shades of blue
no one could misassemble.
One difference between
humans and frogs
is pressure in the lungs,
but I can't say we didn't
have to force the new air in.

WINTER REEDS

I'm not appealing to anything,
here on all fours in the snow,
melt coming through at the knees.
Casual study grown
intense, then forensic,
I face the unexpected
evidence at last: notes
of green mixed into gold
and mold: what lives
lives sick, in keeping
with its time and place.
Windrustle unloading
histories of wordlessness,
I imagine the respiration
of a pheasant I flushed
by accident returning
to normal in a stand
of threadbare hard-
woods twenty yards
away. Twenty years
after he called me
too feeble to get
laid in Tijuana
with a hundred-dollar
bill in my pants,
standing with a woman
money won't buy,
my breath can
come naturally too.

First Hike after Your
Mother's Death

We cross a God-broad field
toward trees, wildflowers
phosphorescing like plankton
in the wake of a great ship,
sign the ranger's check-in
manifest with a pencil
on a string, exchange
breadth for canopy
sunshafts walk through
on long legs when branches
take the wind. Prints
we make in thawing earth
begin to close behind us
before we're out of sight.
The path goes stony, wet
and single file; I watch
you mill your arms to keep
the year's first gnats away,
turn to follow thin squirrels
dashing through new green.
When we pause for juice
and olives amid the fierce
territoriality of butterflies,
you tell me motion unifies
a wind and is its memory,
then move far enough
ahead that you could turn
and see me in the sudden
light as who she wanted
you to settle for, courteous,

with prospects, her choice
not yours. This is where
you disappear into your
new life, but stop and wait
where snowmelt lifts
a sound into the leaves.

BULB

I bring my mother to the green
conservatory grounds.
She stands on a peastone path
between a water feature
and low pine and sniffs the air.
Her eyes are closed,
there's a fragrance
in the wind she wants
to single out and savor,
a curve of scent
that begins elsewhere
and ends elsewhere.
Has nothing yet
been planted
or has nothing
yet appeared?
Joy's bolted
in her face to sorrow
like a pair of shears.

FLEECE

A dam guards the lamb she bore
this morning, looking
fiercer than, I think, most would
think a sheep *could* look.
She doesn't care our hosts
keep her for tax reasons—
she makes their estate a farm—
but if she could she'd care
her charge is overflow.
Commuting to a desk job
I kiss you among strangers
at my nearer stop, leave the silver
train and wedge my way
up packed stairs to the street.
Once upon that flood I turned
and saw you as doors
slid to the sound of a bell
lift a book and clear
space for your reading
with a face as fell.
In unpracticed hands
shears summon blood.
One who followed us
from flutes and wrought
iron on the patio laughs
about naming the lamb
Stew as another sheep
angles its head through
the fence, takes grass
greener than cash in
blunt and slanted teeth.

MONARCH

I snip and keep its leaf moist
indoors on a blue-green
circle of Fiestaware.
In days it darkens and beneath
the dictionary's magnifying
glass a strip of cells
wriggles like a camper
from a tight sleeping bag.
As soon as it can turn
around it conducts mouth-
business with its shell.
I like to think it's
because no mother
visits the same plant
twice that, in nature,
other eggs it finds
are mouthed as well.
Widened by its
origin it riffles
to the leaf edge then
stretches underneath.
In a roof of poison,
it chews holes
through which
I learn to peek.
Of fodder, soon I
wash a sheaf a day,
turn aphids
into golden paste
and rinse them away.
Four times it

pauses long enough
to spin silk anchors
and walk, larger,
from its skin.
Moved to a clear
box, finger–
sized, a fifth
time, dangling,
it whirls a jade
jewel from within.

MENAGERIE

Zoo dromedaries regard us from a distance.
We can't see
the prairie dogs from here.
Soon you'll think you see
a young animal tutored
by an elder of its kind.
But really something
else is happening.
At last I thank you
for pointing out an antelope
months ago. We were
road-tripping, withdrawn
from one another,
having seen what
we came for
different ways.
I don't let you drive
but you took the wheel
with your left hand.
I turned just in time.
It was looking
over a wire fence
at the interstate like
a reader at the end
of a long book
missing its last line.

AUGER

I want to show you a poem
about walking on a frozen lake.
Tired of seeing me reach
for that shelf you've drifted
deeper into the store.
I find a chair in a corner,
keep my thumb on the page.
The Manx cat comes and goes
and the day loses a degree.
Following shapes of wind
in snow we've spoken
sentences between
shores and turned
to find only ellipsis.
Putting the book back
fills a hole in water.
I should find you now
where paper shivers
against your skin
but the cold,
coupling hydrogen
remains too thin.

TARPON, NIGHT DIVE

—Megalops atlanticus

Soundless beside us you blot
a moon dissolved in salt
then give back the light
I shine on you: stainless-
steel eating machine,
the divemaster said,
but you're a hank of muscle
wrapped in chrome.
And you keep pace,
have hot-wired instinct,
learned in less than eons
we illuminate what
interests us and what
interests us tastes
good. Your genus
name means *giant eye*,
yet you teach the art
of looking fast, wait
for us to love a thing
so much we forget
the pendant
shadow of your need.
The reef's bloom
closes at depths
nitrogen makes joy.
When you leave us
you will go that way.

FLYING FISH

Twin Mercuries pull distance from the coast,
making a basin of water,
lifting the prow.
The captain bends his knees in jouncing swells
with such supple reciprocity
he holds the shining wheel
like a newborn's hand.
Bungied cylinders of air groan
against the gunwales.
Moments from the dive site,
vests inflated, fins cinched,
a hodgepodge of pilgrims
parcels lead on belts
to hasten the descent
and slow the climb.
None's not meant
to check another's gear
and share a careful
breathing if need be.
At this speed talk's
torn from mouths
and flung astern.
They're leaning head to head
or gesturing when
the destination leaps
in waves from waves
and comes to them
in spray like blown rain.

HICKEY

We're given bait and shown how to hold it
near the sensitive stingray nose,
a quick briefing—gestural
simulation, really—but weeks
of lecture couldn't prepare us
for the flat host we roll
backward to be loose among.
Pure wing, they follow
our hands so closely
into loops and arcs of scent
we can feel depth relinquished
in the softer of their skins.
How long does it take us
in water sunlight permeates
to forget needing ever to be told?
A stranger swimming
behind us now might think
us part angelic semaphore.
Each diver chooses
differently when to move
the baited hand down
the underneath from the nose
to the mouth of the fish.
It's a question of how
long you can bear taking
advantage of something
more beautiful than yourself,
even if meaning
to feed it in the end.
When we slow and let them
dilate over our open palms

they make a nothing
world in themselves
and suck the old one in.
It can leave
a mark through neoprene.

SALT PIER

Tucked into their feathers twice,
flamingos sleep in wide
evaporation ponds nearby.
We inch our wetsuits on
in headlight beams, hiss
and hoist the heavy tanks,
waddle over rocks and start
to glide. In surface chop,
with words and fingers,
we confirm the compass-
aided out-and-back
we've planned then sink
in marine crackle that
glimmers under pressure
like a ghost of origin.
Tuning buoyancy we hang
alongside pilings smashed
through coral centuries.
Polyps spangle them, life
swarming to the place
of injury, so much so some
come to love the hurt.
You take my hand
above an octopus
tumbling down the reef.
One once clung to you.
A ring of fellow
divers had it trapped
in bars of halogen.
Its ink had failed,

it had to choose.
You spun to shield it
from the light and then,
amorphous in its
urgency, it flew.
I've said for years,
but it's untrue,
that's why we dive
alone, where a live
sea floats the blank
burden of a risen home.

NOTES

The description of the ceremony in "Bullet Ant" came from Wikipedia; its interpretation is my own.

"Ladder" is for John Lawrence.

"Medicine Lake" is for Stuart Friebert.

The larva of the Monarch butterfly eats only leaves from the milkweed plant, which contain a heart-stopping chemical agent. The animal's resultant toxicity is a defense.

ACKNOWLEDGMENTS

Grateful acknowledgement is made to the editors of magazines in which the following pieces first appeared (sometimes in earlier forms):

5 AM: "Bullet Ant," "Coup de Grâce," "Protect and Serve"; *32 Poems:* "Flying Fish"; *Another Chicago Magazine:* "Base Pair"; *Antioch Review:* "It's a Tuesday"; *Boulevard:* "Express," "Ornament"; *Carolina Quarterly:* "Beach Thanksgiving," "Boboli Slope"; *Cloudbank:* "Medicine Lake"; *FIELD:* "Aubade," "Auger," "Bulb," "First Hike after Your Mother's Death," "Glass," "Hickey," "The Painted Hall, Lascaux," "Rake," "Song," "Stepfather," "Umpire," "Ward," "Winter Reeds"; *Greensboro Review:* "Pulp"; *Manchester Review* (UK): "Green Zone"; *Margie:* "Sever"; *Mudfish:* "The Value of Literature"; *Mudlark:* "Balance"; *New Letters:* "Quail"; *Plume:* "Menagerie"; *Poet Lore:* "Ladder"; *Poetry:* "Turkey Fallen Dead from Tree"; *Quarterly West:* "Apology"; *Redivider:* "Dart"; *Salt Hill:* "Grunion"; *Sonora Review:* "Frame," "Cleave"; *South Carolina Review:* "Infection"; *Southern Indiana Review:* "Fleece"; *Talking River Review:* "Magnifying Glass."

"Aubade" also appeared in *American Life in Poetry*. "Grunion" also appeared on *Verse Daily*. "Quail" also appeared on *Poetry Daily* and *Verse Daily*. "Noninvasive" first appeared in *The Bridport Prize Anthology 2009*, and also appeared in *Evolver* (UK) and the Minneapolis *Star Tribune*. "First Hike after Your Mother's Death" and "The Painted Hall, Lascaux" also appeared in *The Hecht Prize Anthology—2005–2009*.

The epigraph by Franz Wright is taken from *Kindertotenwald* (Knopf, 2011).

My teachers have included David Young, Diane Vreuls, James Galvin, Pamela Alexander, and Gerald Stern. Special guidance has come from Thomas Lux and David Walker. Stuart Friebert has provided boon companionship, close readings, and moral support for years. Anything worth it, they've helped save.

I thank the U.S. Department of Education for a Jacob K. Javits Fellowship that kept me in school.

I thank Linda Gregerson and Ed Ochester.

I thank my family.